D1826073

A PHOTO JOURNAL
BEACH
S BOOKS

RANGER

RANGER

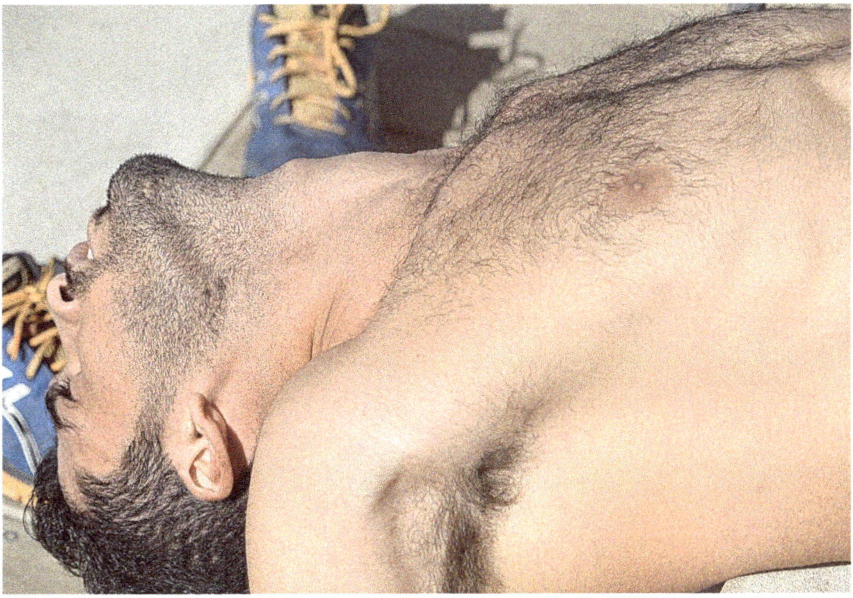

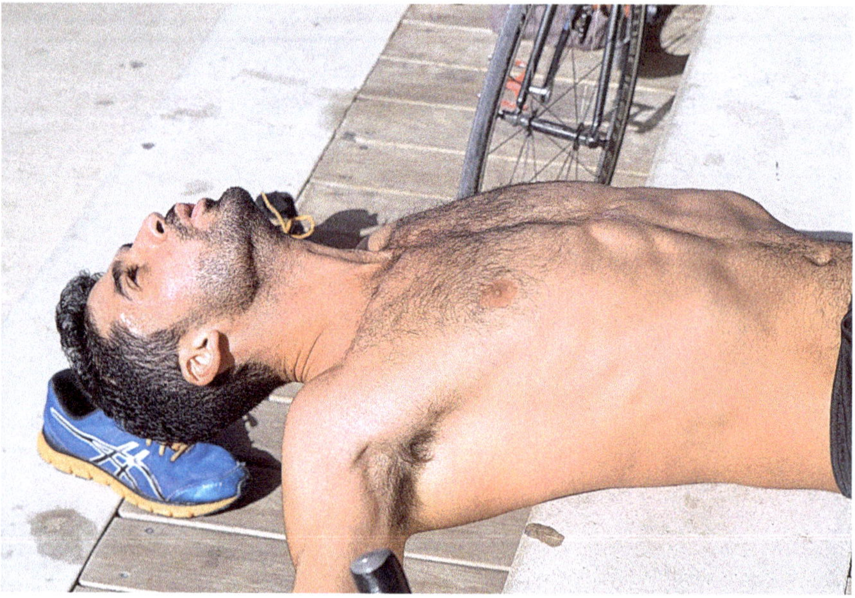

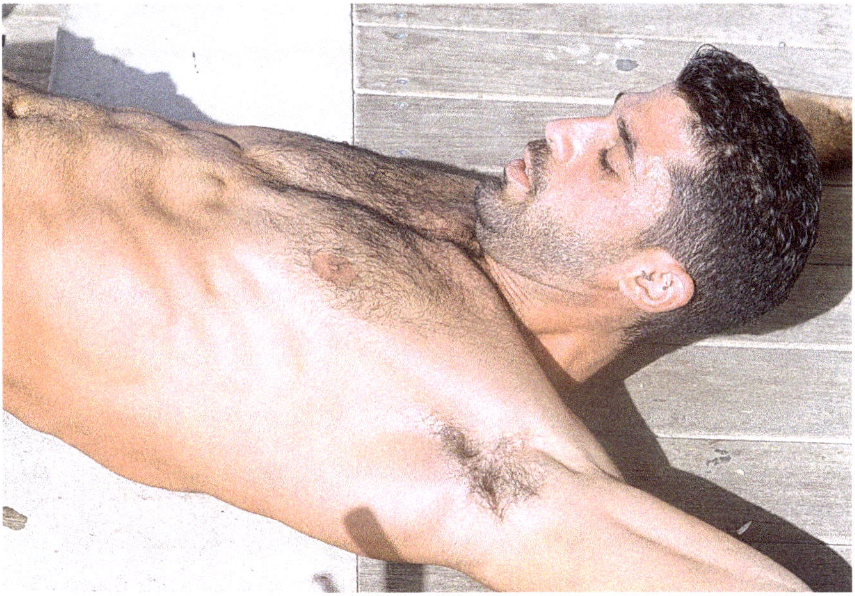

technoLayer

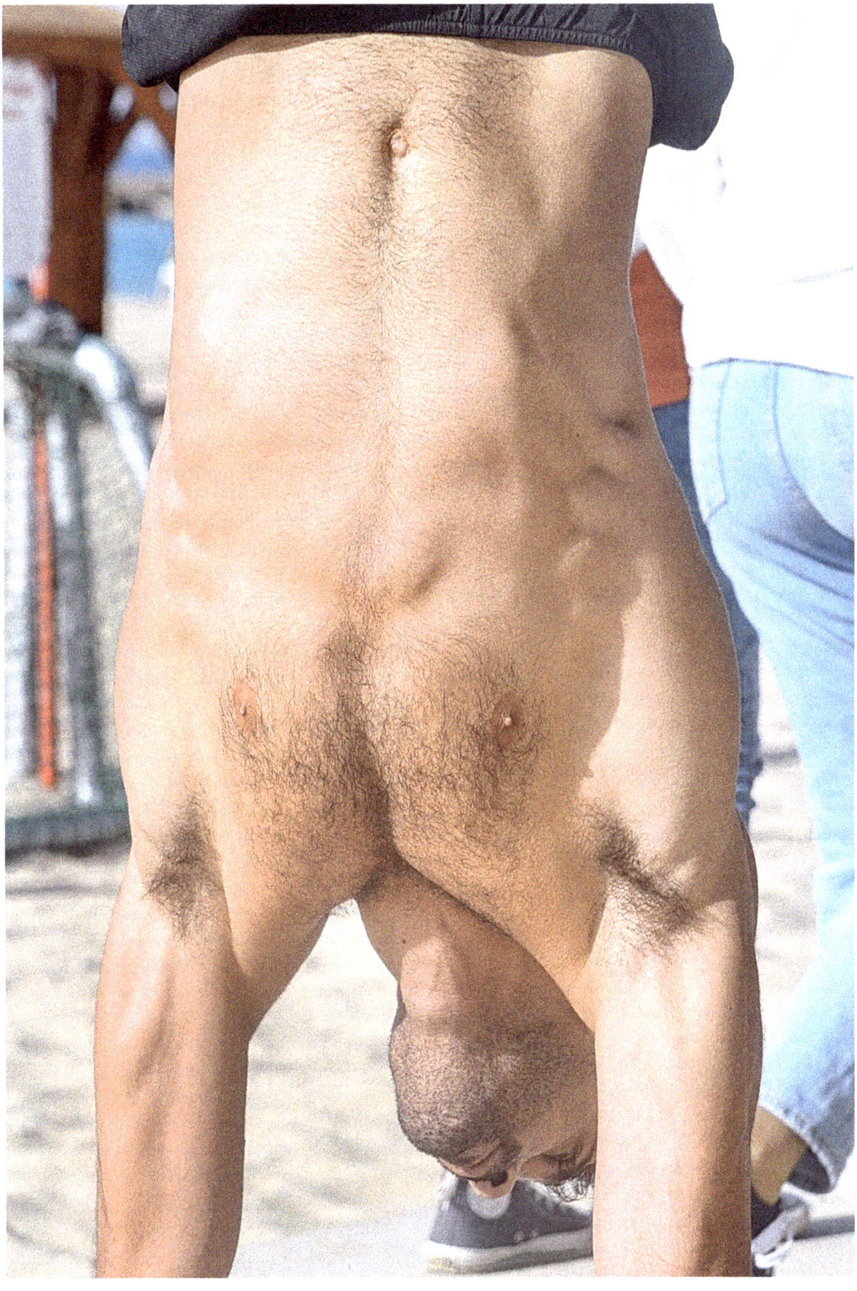

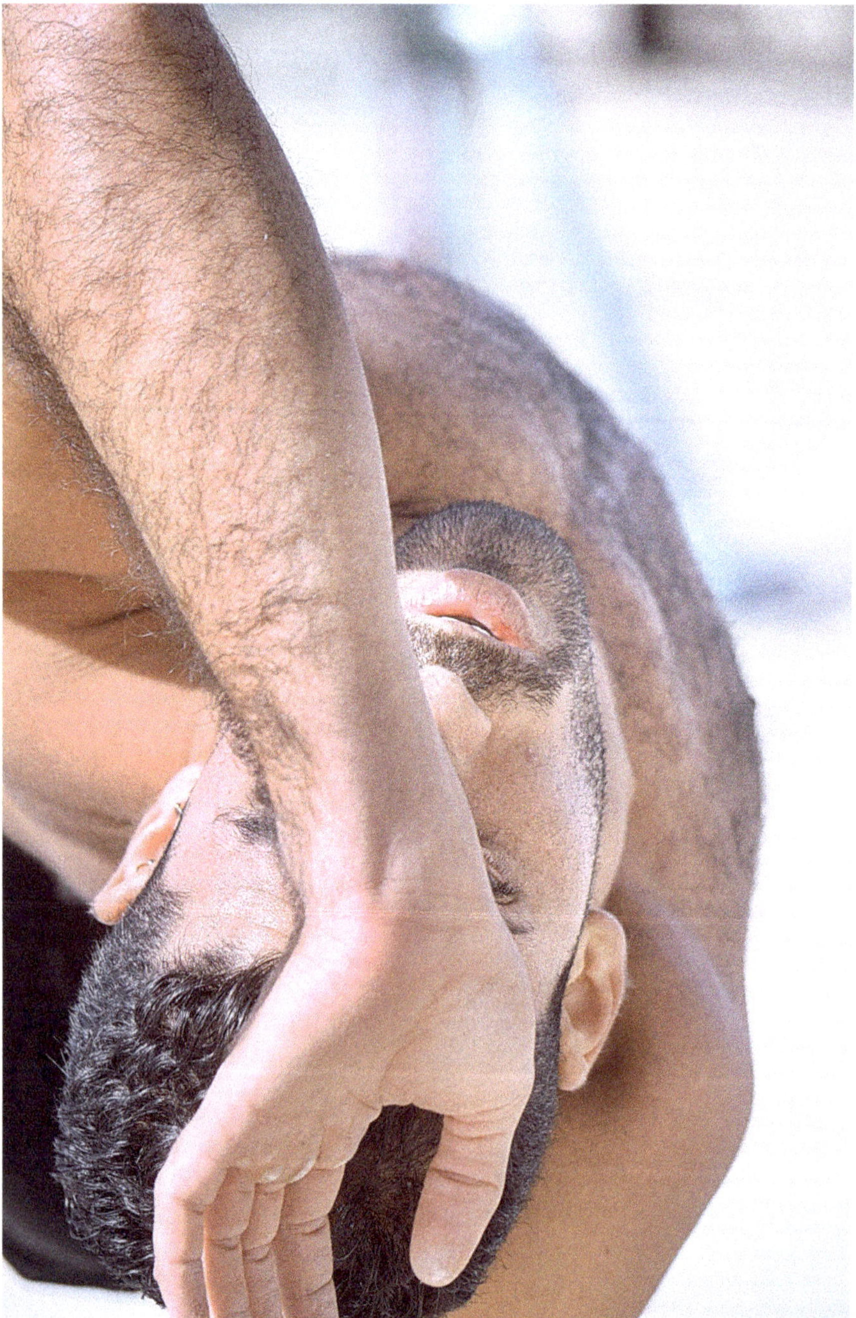

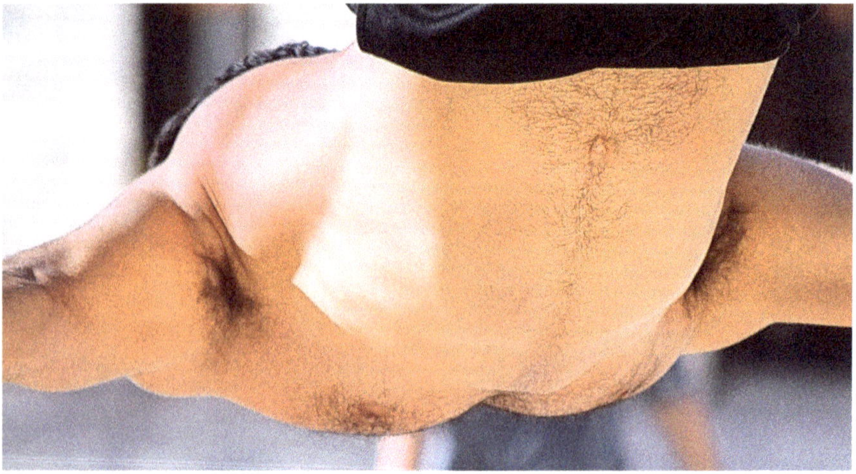

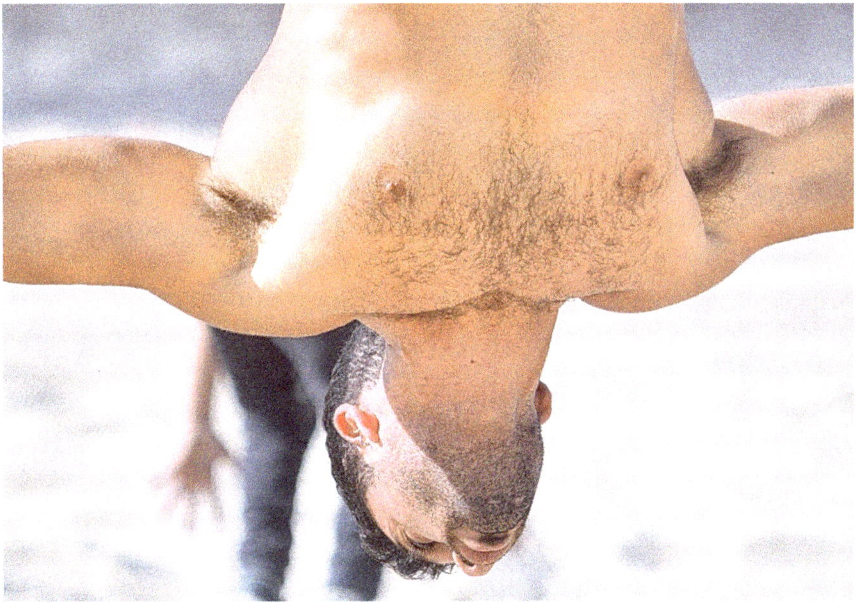

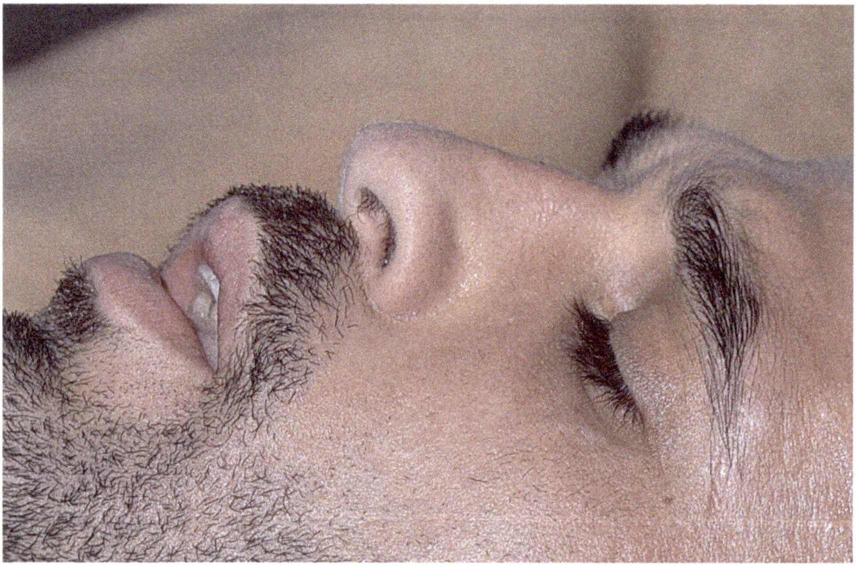

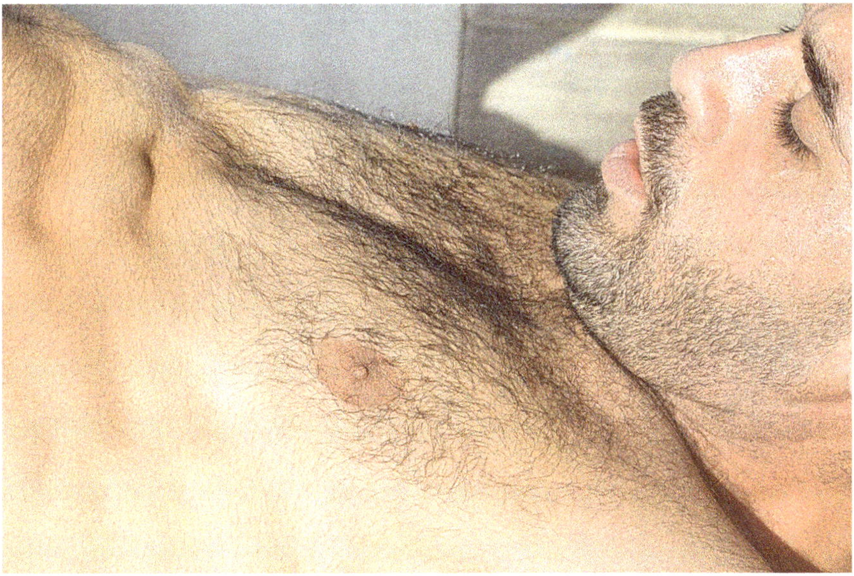

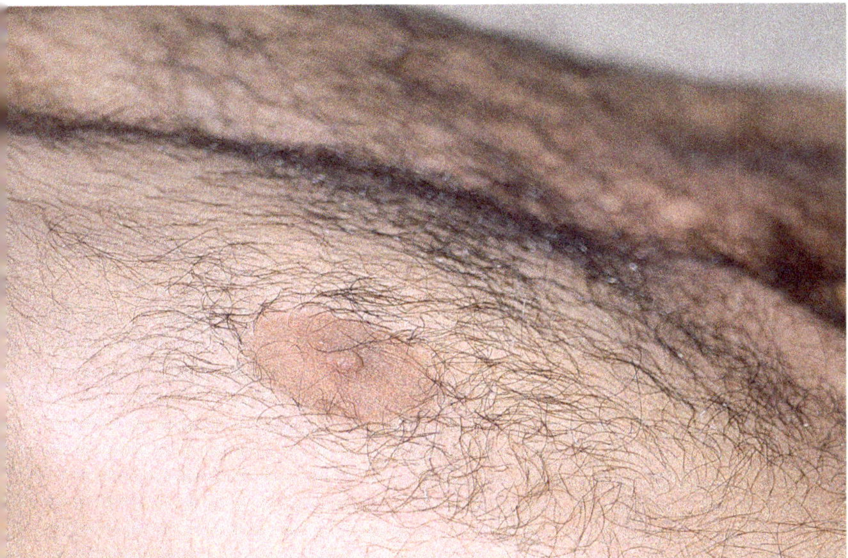

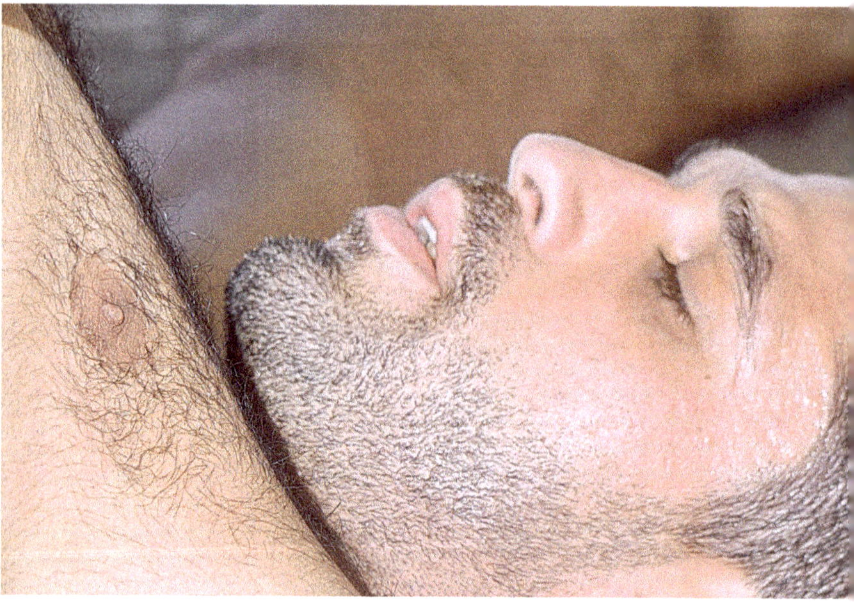

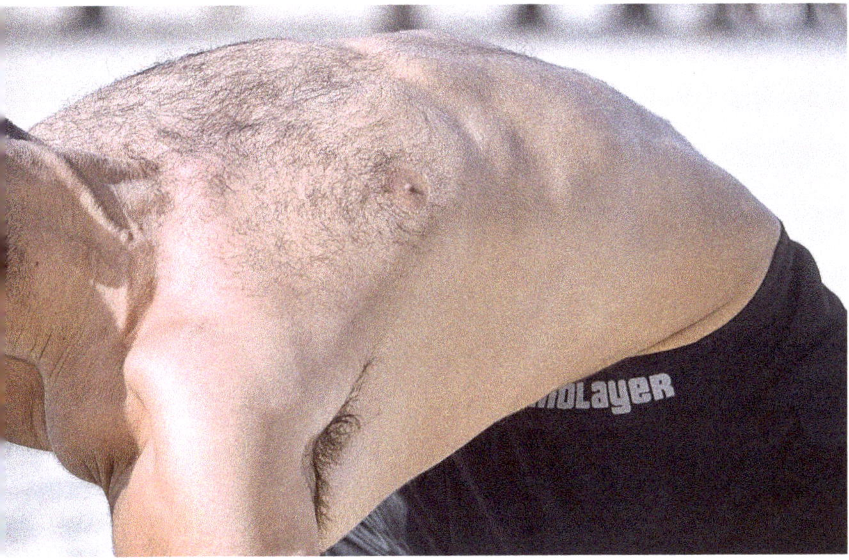

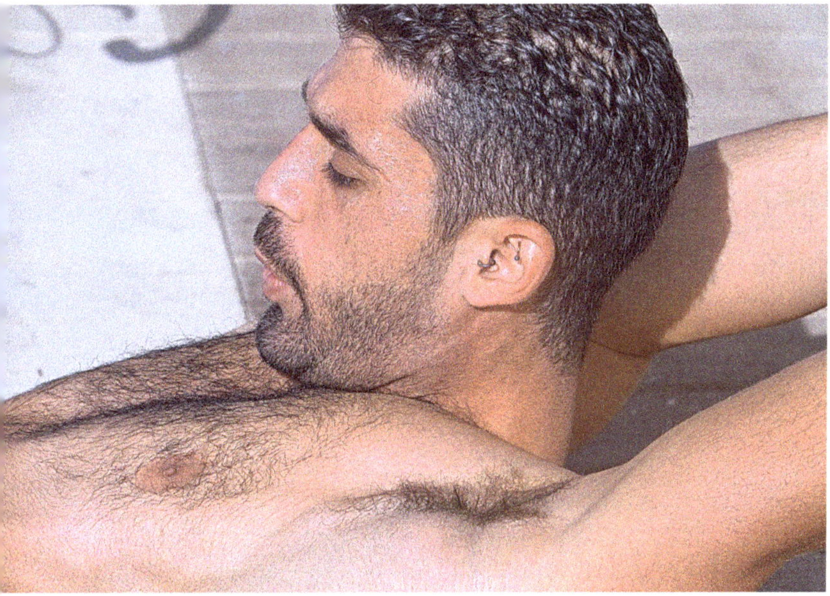

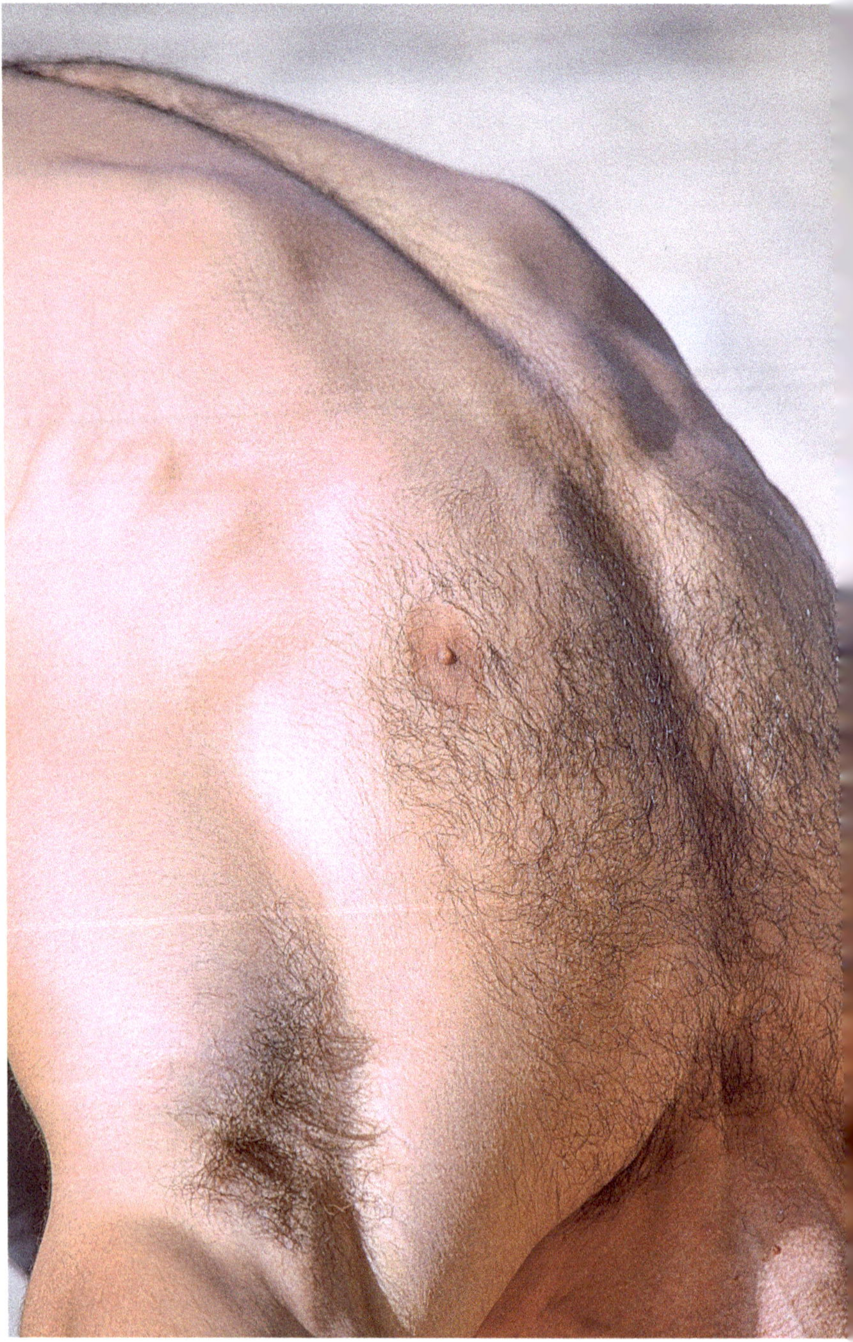

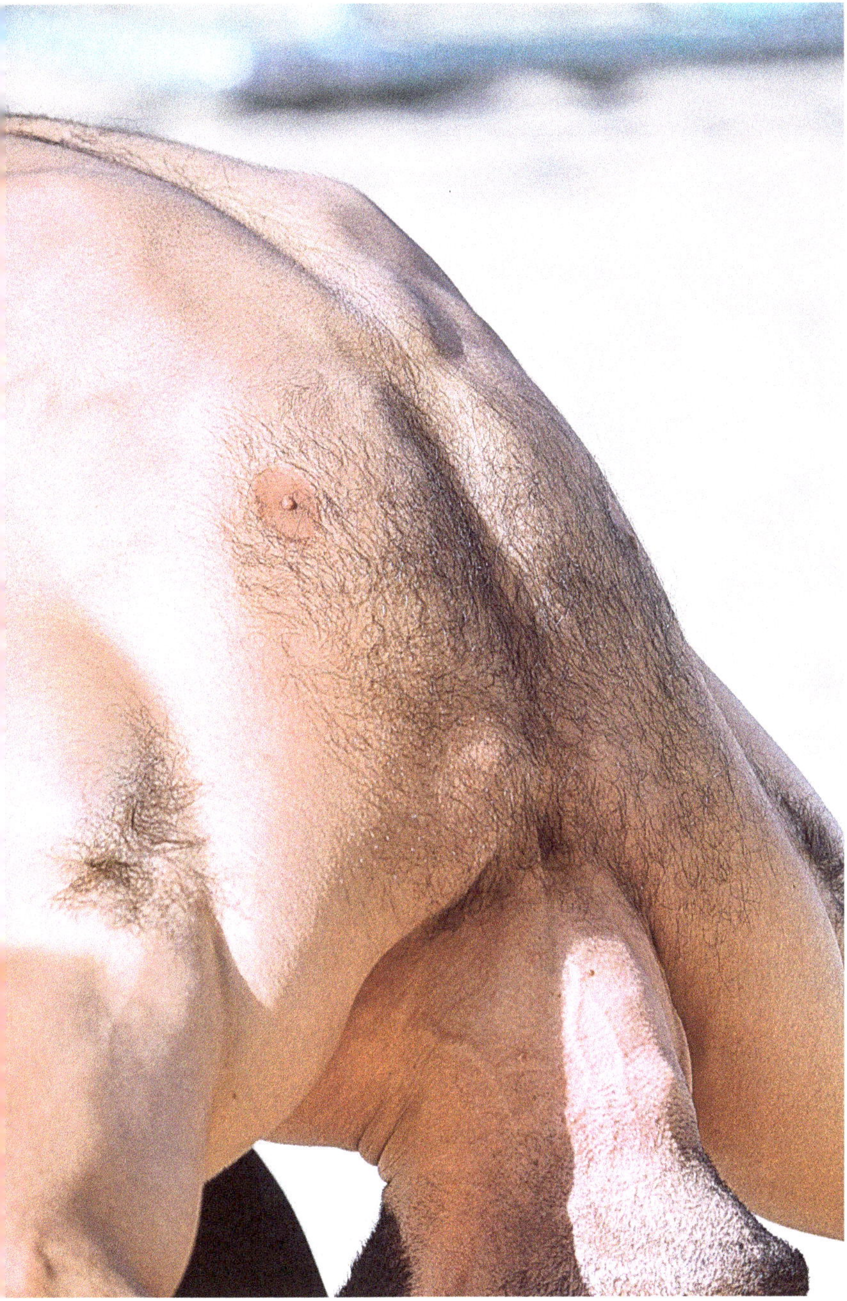

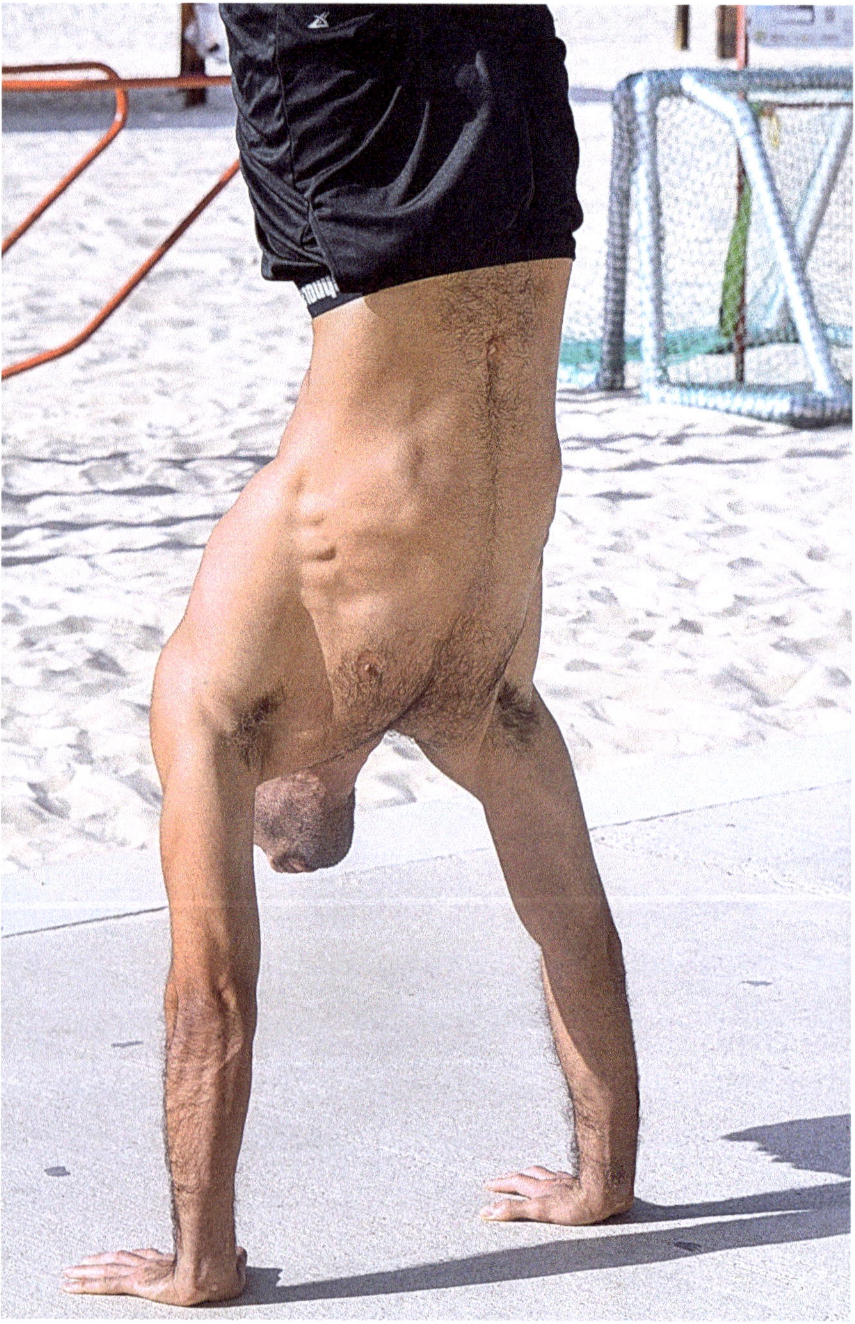

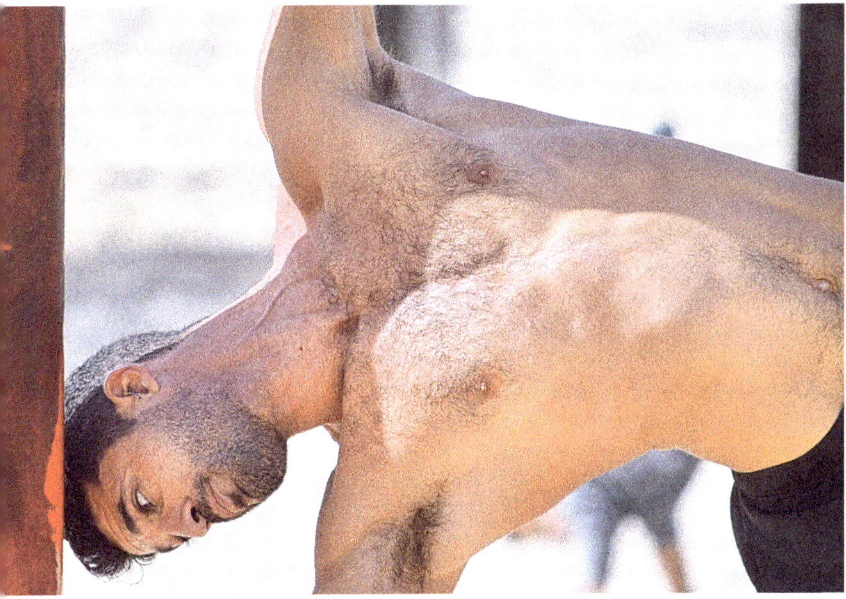

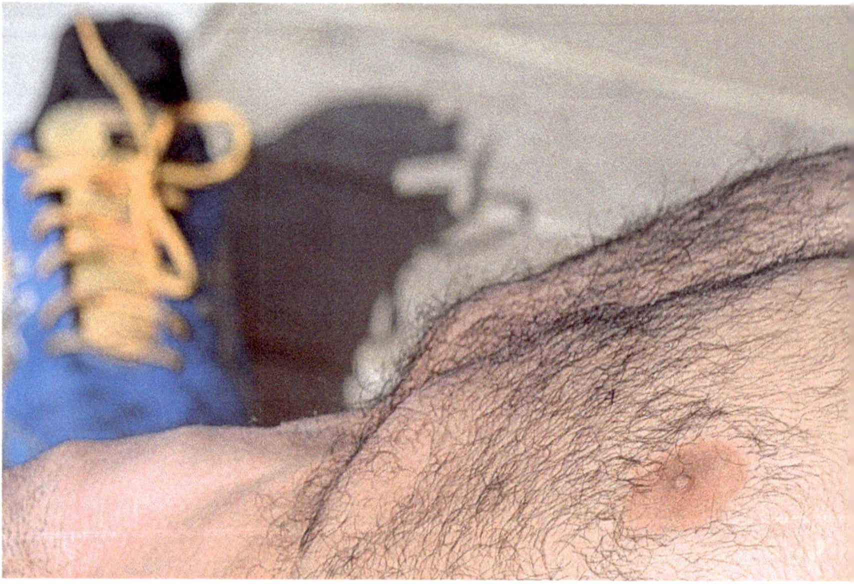

technoLayer

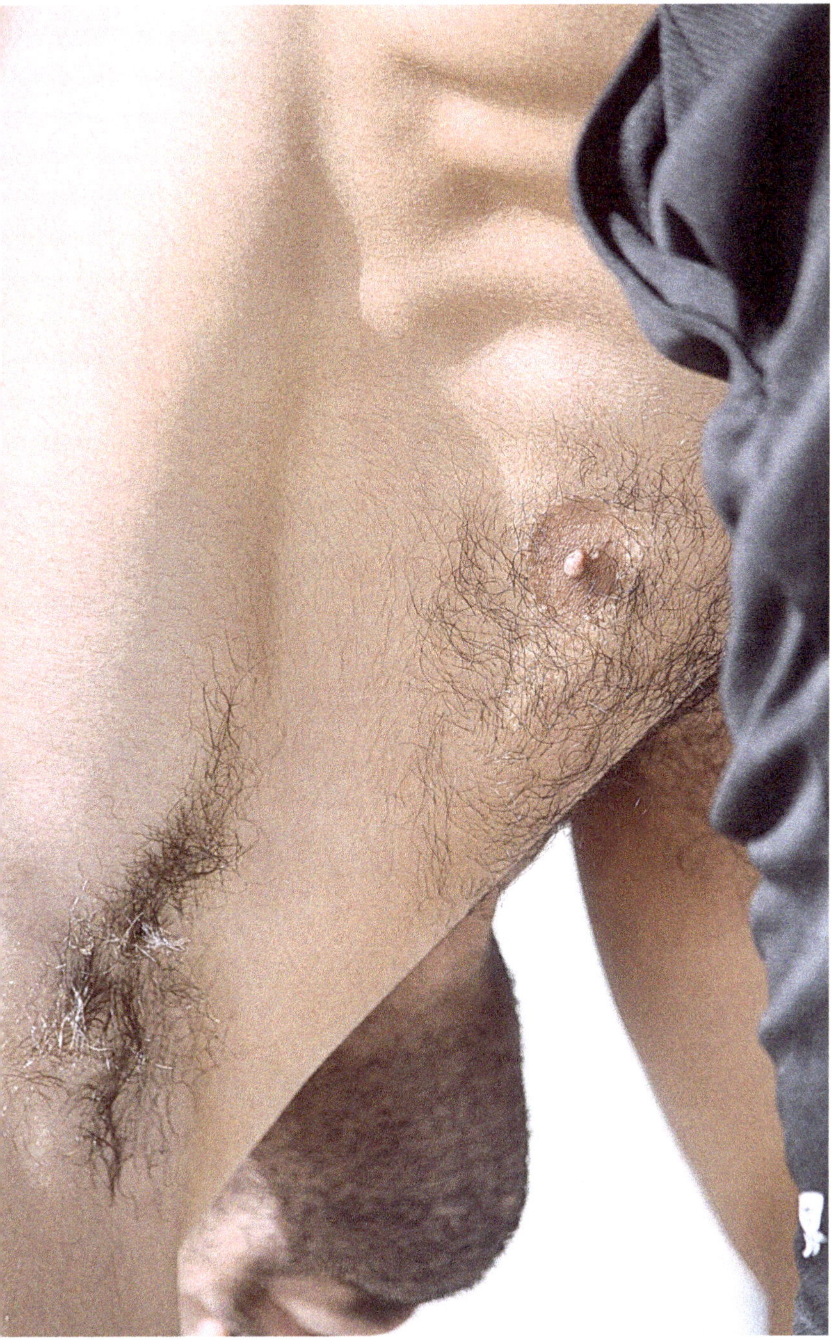

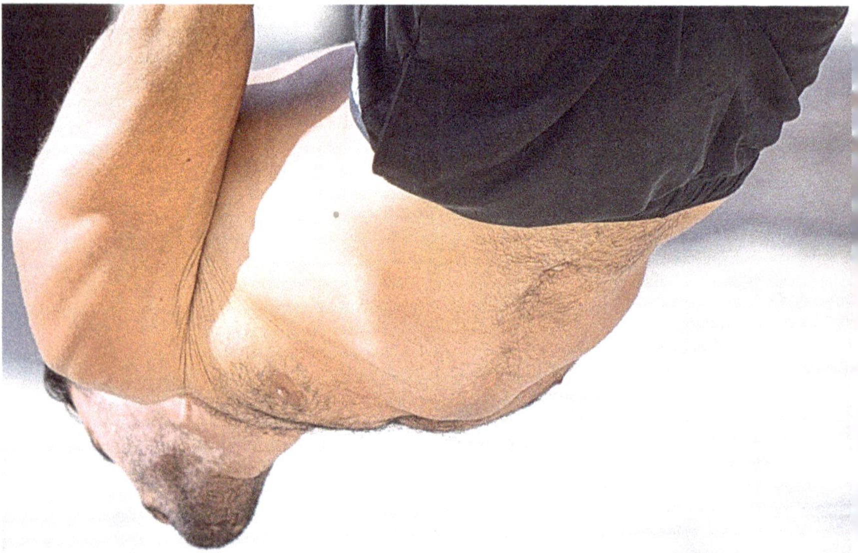

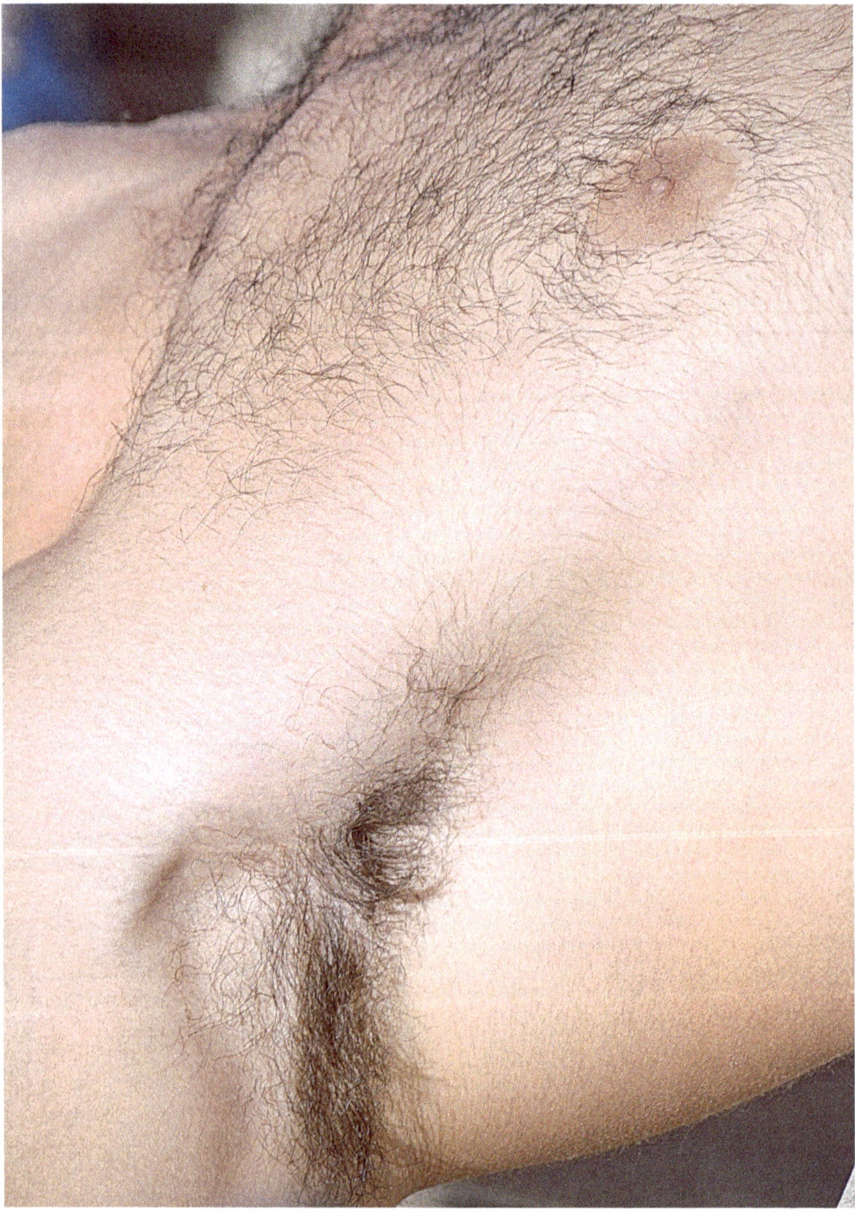

speedo

Lightning Source UK Ltd.
Milton Keynes UK
UKHW020009240119
335948UK00002B/20/P

9 780368 137921